Classic Recipes of
FRANCE

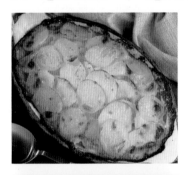

Classic Recipes of
FRANCE

TRADITIONAL FOOD AND COOKING
IN 25 AUTHENTIC DISHES

CAROLE CLEMENTS &
ELIZABETH WOLF-COHEN

LORENZ BOOKS

This edition is published by
Lorenz Books,
an imprint of Anness Publishing Ltd,
Blaby Road, Wigston, LE18 4SE

www.lorenzbooks.com;
www.annesspublishing.com

© Anness Publishing Limited 2013

If you like the images in this book and
would like to investigate using them
for publishing, promotions or
advertising, please visit our website
www.practicalpictures.com for more
information.

Publisher: Joanna Lorenz
Editor: Helen Sudell
Designer: Nigel Partridge
Production Controller: Steve Lang
Recipe Photography: Amanda
 Heywood

The image on the front cover is of
Chocolate Profiteroles, page 60

A CIP catalogue record for this book
is available from the British Library

Publisher's Note:
Although the advice and information
in this book are believed to be
accurate and true at the time of going
to press, neither the authors nor the
publisher can accept any legal
responsibility or liability for any errors
or omissions that may have been
made nor for any inaccuracies nor for
any loss, harm or injury that comes
about from following instructions or
advice in this book.

The Publisher would like to thank the
following agencies for the use of their
images. iStockphoto: p6, 8, 9, 10.

Cook's Notes
Bracketed terms are intended for
American readers. For all recipes,
quantities are given in both metric and
imperial measures and, where
appropriate, in standard cups and
spoons. Follow one set of measures,
but not a mixture, because they are
not interchangeable.

Standard spoon and cup measures
are level. 1 tsp = 5ml, 1 tbsp = 15ml,
1 cup = 250ml/8fl oz. Australian
standard tablespoons are 20ml.
Australian readers should use 3 tsp in
place of 1 tbsp for measuring small
quantities.

American pints are 16fl oz/2 cups.
American readers should use 20fl
oz/2.5 cups in place of 1 pint when
measuring liquids.

Electric oven temperatures in this
book are for conventional ovens.
When using a fan oven, the
temperature will probably need to be
reduced by about 10–20°C/20–40°F.
Since ovens vary, you should check
with your manufacturer's instruction
book for guidance.

The nutritional analysis given for each
recipe is calculated per portion (i.e.
serving or item), unless otherwise
stated. If the recipe gives a range,
such as Serves 4–6, then the
nutritional analysis will be for the
smaller portion size, i.e. 6 servings.
The analysis does not include optional
ingredients, ie salt added to taste.

Medium (US large) eggs are used
unless otherwise stated.

Contents

Introduction

The cuisine of France is deservedly admired the world over. What makes it so special is French people's attitude to food. They take great pride in the skills of their chefs, cheesemakers, bakers and winemakers and have a real reverence for good basic ingredients, taking trouble to seek out the freshest and best-quality basic foods. France is known for its haute cuisine – elaborate recipes prepared by skilful chefs in top restaurants – but more representative of the country's gastronomy is traditional home cooking, which tends to be simple but makes superb use of the finest seasonal ingredients.

This book celebrates the best of traditional French cooking with classic recipes from all over the country.

Left: A typically rural scene of vineyards in the foothills of the Vosges mountains, Alsace. France is famed for its wine making and produces some of the world's finest wines.

French Cuisine

The joys of the table are everything to the French and fundamental to their way of life. Food is a constant source of conversation, talked about everywhere, on the Metro, in shops, in the office and at the school gate. In France, family meals are an occasion. An everyday event becomes a celebration of one of life's most basic pleasures, and special parties, birthdays and holidays are lavishly enjoyed with food and wine.

Below: French beef is revered throughout the world.

Above: Wine, bread, olive oil and herbs are always at the centre of french cuisine.

French cuisine is universally revered and is often seen as a benchmark for the cooking of other countries. But what makes it so special? Part of what distinguishes French cuisine is simply the attitude of the French towards food.

France is and always has been primarily an agricultural economy and fresh seasonal ingredients are widely available. In the past, the French would shop twice a day for the two main meals. The constraints of modern life have brought change but it is characteristic that the French are still prepared to spend time seeking out fine fresh products, rather than stocking up on processed food.

Similarly, the classic techniques of French cooking have been developed with a high regard for the ingredients. The French cook takes as much care and attention over the preparation of an onion as to the cooking of exotic shellfish.

However, the repertoire of techniques that forms the foundation of French cooking is not as extensive as you might think. Its variety and finesse rest on a relatively small number of basic techniques. For example, sautéed chicken breasts with a wine and cream sauce require essentially the same cooking method as pan-fried trout with a lemon and butter sauce.

Right: The French love to shop for fresh local ingredients in market stalls, which are at the very heart of the French way of living and cooking.

Left: A sprinkling of fresh herbs adds flavour and intensity.

The French style of serving a meal differs from many other countries and for foreigners part of the enjoyment of French food is in eating 'the French way' – in separate courses. Whether it is a fresh egg perfectly fried in butter or an extravagantly rich layered meringue cake, each part of a meal is meant to be savoured separately.

Today, as in the past, most French people still consider the midday meal the main event of the day, although the demands of modern urban life make it often more difficult to realize. Whenever possible the French

will take the time to sit down to lunch. An informal family meal is likely to be two courses, an appetizer and a main course, plus cheese and perhaps fresh fruit. If a dessert is served, the starter will be very light, but it is rarely omitted.

Typically, the appetizer sets the tone for the rest of the meal. Cooked vegetables, such as asparagus or artichokes with a flavourful dressing, or a slice of ham or pâté from the local charcuterie, are popular, as are composed salads or crudités. Soup has always been a traditional first course at supper,

perhaps followed by a vegetable gratin or quiche. Egg and cheese dishes make more substantial appetizers and may also be served as a light lunch or as a main course for supper.

A rich or filling appetizer should be followed by a more spartan main course, such as steamed or poached fish. A plain green salad is often served with or after the main course, followed by a cheese course. Elaborate desserts are reserved for special celebrations, and

Below: Vineyards grow in many regions of France and the French are proud of their wine.

Above: The French are very partial to their fancy cakes.

with the superb creations available in pâtisseries, the dessert is more often bought than home-made.

Formal French menus are more complex and offer five or sometimes more courses. The meal might start with, for instance, a shellfish hors d'oeuvre, followed by a fish course, then a roast of meat or poultry, cheese and finally a dessert. Petits fours, small cakes and sweetmeats, might be offered with the coffee.

Restaurants often feature a menu de dégustation, a sort of sampler meal with multiple small courses highlighting the chef's specialities.

Sauces are perhaps the best known elements of French cuisine. The union of good ingredients and a skilfully made sauce elevates the simplest of dishes. A sauce can be as quick and easy as deglazing a pan with a little wine, or more elaborate, such as Béarnaise. Either way, the point is to make the food taste even better.

A good sauce should enhance food and not disguise it and similarly some thought must be given to balancing the courses. A starter of asparagus with hollandaise should not be followed by chicken breasts with a creamy sauce – a simple pan-fried sole or grilled (broiled) lamb chop would be preferable.

For the French, wine is an integral part of the meal. Just as a sauce is made to complement the meat or vegetable it accompanies, so the wines are chosen to complement the whole meal. Many of the world's great wines come from France and French wine, like French cuisine, remains the standard for all others. In wine-producing regions people drink the wines of that area, and these wines almost invariably enhance the regional foods. In areas where wine is not produced, as in Normandy and Brittany, the local products – apples and pears – are made into other drinks, such as sparkling dry cider.

You don't have to live in France to cook and eat 'the French way' and this book's range of tempting recipes will help to get you started.

Below: Making a good sauce is an essential skill to acquire.

Classic Ingredients

The key words are 'fresh' and 'top-quality' when it comes to selecting ingredients for French cooking at home.

Fish and seafood

With its long coastlines and many freshwater rivers and lakes, it is no wonder the French enjoy their fish. The firm, white, meaty flesh of monkfish holds its shape well during cooking. Red mullet

Below: Many families in rural areas will keep chickens to have fresh eggs readily available.

is often grilled or baked whole. The firm, pink flesh of salmon suits most cooking methods, and the highly esteemed turbot has a tasty, white flesh that may be steamed, fried or grilled.

Very versatile, the humble prawn (shrimp) combines well with many other kinds of fish, and is a key ingredient in the classic fish stew Bouillabaisse. Available all year round, mussels have a wonderful, fragrant flavour. The sweet-tasting and more meatier shellfish, scallops, are equally revered.

Above: Red mullet offers a true taste of the Mediterranean.

Chicken and meat

The young and tender cornfed roasting chicken is popular in many French dishes, notably Coq au Vin and Chicken Kiev.

The French use various cooking methods for beef, depending on the cut, but one of the best-known is the *daube*, in which it is braised slowly in the oven with wine and herbs. The leg and best end of neck (*carré*) of lamb are enjoyed roasted, often with pulses such as haricot beans or Puy lentils.

Right: Ham, sausages and steak are all popular French meats.

Above: Goat's cheese is enjoyed grilled in salads and tarts.

Fresh (as opposed to cured), succulent pork combines wonderfully with products from Normandy, such as cream, apples and Calvados, and also makes delicious pâtés.

Made from coarsely cut pork, Toulouse sausages are used in cassoulets, but can also be simply fried or grilled.

Dairy Products

French cooking makes full use of milk, butter, cream and crème fraîche. They give a rich, creamy texture and flavour to soups, casseroles and desserts.

France is renowned for its vast range of cheeses made from cow's, ewe's and goat's milk, and eggs are essential for that most versatile of Gallic fast foods, the omelette, and of course, the soufflé.

Vegetables & Salads

The French are rightly proud of their fresh vegetables and use a vast array of them in their cooking. The vegetables that can be relied upon to bring flavour to any savoury dish are garlic, onions, shallots and

Below: Mushrooms add an earthy flavour to casseroles.

Above: Tomatoes and onions form the basis for many sauces.

leeks, while fresh-flavoured (bell) peppers are an essential ingredient in many dishes.

Versatile, delicious and colourful, just-ripe tomatoes are used in salads and cooked dishes as well as forming the base to many sauces.

With their rich, earthy flavour, wild mushrooms are used extensively. The most prized are chanterelles, morels and ceps. A crisp, aniseed-flavoured, bulb-like vegetable, fennel goes well with fish.

Resembling a large thistle head, the bottom part of the globe artichoke's leaves and the tender heart are edible, but the

Above: Black olives are used in many Mediterranean dishes.

Above: Raspberries are a key fruit in many desserts.

Saffron is used in fish dishes like Bouillabaisse. *Quatre épices* (a mixture of ground cloves, cinnamon, nutmeg and pepper) gives a lift to meat pâtés.

Flavourings & Chocolate

Generous use is made of red and white wine in French cuisine, while liqueurs such as pastis and Calvados make desserts irresistible. Red and white wine vinegars are used for savoury dishes and salads. French chocolatiers are highly skilled and create recipes that prove that dark (bittersweet) and white chocolate make sumptuous desserts.

hairy "choke" is discarded. Black olives are used often in southern French cooking for stuffings, sauces, stews and the pâté known as Tapenade.

Fruit

Grown in abundance, apples are used in both savoury and sweet dishes. Enjoyed in the summer, raspberries, strawberries and blueberries are often eaten in chilled desserts.

Citrus fruit, such as oranges and lemons, feature in savoury and sweet dishes. Oranges are a key ingredient of the spectacular flambéed dessert Crêpes Suzette with Cointreau.

Herbs & Aromatics

French cuisine makes copious use of fresh green herbs, including parsley, basil, dill, thyme, sorrel, marjoram, bay, chervil, tarragon and chives.

Below: A classic bouquet garni: sprigs of bay, thyme and parsley.

Below: Only use good quality chocolate for the best results.

A rich culinary heritage

With its miles of coastline, high mountain peaks, long, rambling rivers and huge swathes of rich agricultural land, the French countryside offers variety and contrast, with a rich array of home-grown fruit and vegetables. Every region has its own specialities which reflect the local products and traditions but the essence of really good French food is its simplicity – bringing out the best in the ingredients to hand. From timeless soups and appetizing light meals to robust meat casseroles and luscious desserts, cakes and bakes, this special collection of authentic recipes aims to unlock the secrets of French cuisine for the home cook.

Left: Locally grown apples and pears are used by French cooks when making their desserts and pastries.

French Onion Soup
Soupe à l'Oignon Gratinée

Serves 6–8

15g/½oz/1 tbsp butter
30ml/2 tbsp olive oil
4 large onions (about 675g/1½lb),
  thinly sliced
2–4 garlic cloves, finely chopped,
  plus 1 whole clove for the toasted
  bread
5ml/1 tsp sugar
2.5ml/½ tsp dried thyme
30ml/2 tbsp plain (all-purpose) flour
125ml/4fl oz/½ cup dry white wine
2 litres/3⅓ pints/8 cups chicken or
  beef stock
30ml/2 tbsp brandy (optional)
6–8 thick slices French bread,
  toasted
340g/12oz Gruyère or Emmenthal
  cheese, grated

1 In a large heavy pan or flameproof casserole, heat the butter and oil over a medium-high heat. Add the onions and cook for 10–12 minutes until they are softened and beginning to brown. Add the garlic, sugar and thyme and continue cooking over a medium heat for 30–35 minutes until the onions are well browned, stirring frequently.

2 Sprinkle over the flour and stir until well blended. Stir in the white wine and stock and bring to the boil. Skim off any foam that rises to the surface, then reduce the heat and simmer gently for 45 minutes. Stir in the brandy, if using.

3 Preheat the grill (broiler). Rub each slice of toasted French bread with the garlic clove. Place six or eight ovenproof soup bowls on a baking sheet and fill about three-quarters full with the onion soup.

4 Float a piece of toast in each bowl. Top with grated cheese, dividing it evenly, and grill (broil) about 15cm/6in from the heat for about 3–4 minutes until the cheese begins to melt and bubble.

This standard French bistro fare is served so frequently, it is simply referred to as gratinée.

Wild Mushroom Soup
Velouté de Champignons Sauvages

Serves 6–8

30g/1oz dried wild mushrooms, such as morels, ceps or porcini
1.5 litres/2½ pints/6 cups chicken stock
30g/1oz/2 tbsp butter
2 onions, coarsely chopped
2 garlic cloves, chopped
900g/2lb button (white) mushrooms, trimmed and sliced
2.5ml/½ tsp dried thyme
1.5ml/¼ tsp freshly grated nutmeg
30–45ml/2–3 tbsp plain (all-purpose) flour
125ml/4fl oz/½ cup dry sherry
125ml/4fl oz/½ cup crème fraîche
salt and freshly ground black pepper
chopped fresh chives, to garnish

In France, many people still pick their own wild mushrooms, from fields and forest, taking them to the local chemist to be checked before using them in all sorts of delicious dishes.

1 Rinse the dried mushrooms under cold running water, shaking to remove as much sand as possible. Place them in a pan with 250ml/8fl oz/1 cup of the stock and bring to the boil over a medium-high heat. Remove the pan from the heat and set aside for 30–40 minutes to soak.

2 Meanwhile, in a flameproof casserole, melt the butter. Add the onions and cook for 5–7 minutes until they are well softened and just golden.

3 Stir in the garlic and fresh mushrooms and cook for 4–5 minutes until they begin to soften, then add the salt and pepper, thyme and nutmeg and flour. Cook for 3–5 minutes, stirring frequently, until well blended.

4 Add the sherry, the remaining chicken stock, the dried mushrooms and their soaking liquid and cook, covered, for 30–40 minutes until the mushrooms are very tender.

5 Purée the soup in batches. Strain it back into the pan, pressing firmly to force the purée through. Stir in the crème fraîche and sprinkle with the chopped chives just before serving.

Provençal Vegetable Soup Soupe au Pistou

Serves 6–8

275g/10oz/1½ cups fresh broad
   (fava) beans, shelled, or
   175g/6oz/¾ cup dried haricot
   (navy) beans, soaked overnight
2.5ml/½ tsp dried herbes de
   Provence
2 garlic cloves, finely chopped
15ml/1 tbsp olive oil
1 onion, finely chopped
2 small or 1 large leek, finely sliced
1 celery stick, finely sliced
2 carrots, finely diced
2 small potatoes, finely diced
120g/4oz green beans
1.2 litres/2 pints/5 cups water
120g/4oz/1 cup shelled garden peas,
   fresh or frozen
2 small courgettes (zucchini), finely
   chopped
3 medium tomatoes, peeled, seeded
   and finely chopped
handful of spinach leaves, cut into
   thin ribbons
sprigs of fresh basil, to garnish

For the pistou

1 or 2 garlic cloves, finely chopped
15g/½oz/½ cup basil leaves
60ml/4 tbsp grated Parmesan
   cheese
60 ml/4 tbsp extra virgin olive oil

1 To make the *pistou*, put the garlic, basil and Parmesan cheese in a food processor and process until smooth, scraping down the sides once. With the machine running, slowly add the olive oil through the feed tube. Or, alternatively, pound the garlic, basil and cheese in a mortar and pestle and stir in the oil.

2 To make the soup, if using dried haricot beans, place them in a pan and cover with water. Boil vigorously for 10 minutes and drain. Place the par-boiled beans, or fresh beans if using, in a pan with the herbes de Provence and one of the garlic cloves. Add water to cover by 2.5cm/1in. Bring to the boil, reduce the heat and simmer over a medium-low heat until tender, about 10 minutes for fresh beans and about 1 hour for dried beans. Set aside in the cooking liquid.

3 Heat the oil in a large pan. Add the onion and leeks, and cook for 5 minutes, stirring occasionally, until the onion just softens.

4 Add the celery, carrots and the other garlic clove and cook, covered, for 10 minutes, stirring.

5 Add the potatoes, green beans and water, then season lightly with salt and pepper. Bring to the boil, skimming any foam that rises to the surface, then reduce the heat, cover and simmer gently for 10 minutes.

6 Add the peas, courgettes and tomatoes together with the reserved beans and their cooking liquid and simmer for 25–30 minutes, or until all the vegetables are tender. Add the spinach and simmer for 5 minutes. Season the soup and swirl a spoonful of *pistou* into each bowl. Garnish with basil and serve.

This satisfying soup captures all the flavours of a summer in Provence. The basil and garlic purée, pistou, *gives it extra colour and a wonderful aroma – so don't omit it.*

Goat's Cheese Soufflé
Soufflé au Fromage de Chèvre

Serves 4–6

30g/1oz/2 tbsp butter
30g/1oz/3 tbsp plain (all-purpose) flour
175ml/6fl oz/¾ cup milk
1 bay leaf
freshly grated nutmeg
grated Parmesan cheese, for sprinkling
40g/1½oz herb and garlic soft cheese
150g/5oz firm goat's cheese, diced
6 egg whites, at room temperature
1.5ml/¼ tsp cream of tartar
salt and freshly ground black pepper

1 Melt the butter in a heavy pan over a medium heat. Add the flour and cook until slightly golden, stirring occasionally. Pour in half the milk, stirring vigorously until smooth, then stir in the remaining milk and add the bay leaf. Season with a pinch of salt and plenty of pepper and nutmeg. Reduce the heat to medium-low, cover and simmer gently for about 5 minutes, stirring occasionally.

2 Preheat the oven to 190°C/ 375°F/ Gas 5. Generously butter a 1.5 litre/2½ pint soufflé dish and sprinkle with Parmesan cheese.

3 Remove the sauce from the heat and discard the bay leaf. Stir in both the cheeses.

4 In a clean greasefree bowl, using an electric mixer or balloon whisk, beat the egg whites slowly until they become frothy. Add the cream of tartar, increase the speed and continue beating until they form soft peaks, then stiffer peaks that just flop over a little at the top.

5 Stir a spoonful of beaten egg whites into the cheese sauce to lighten it, then pour the cheese sauce over the remaining whites. Using a rubber spatula or large metal spoon, gently fold the sauce into the whites until the mixtures are just combined, cutting down through the centre to the bottom, then along the side of the bowl and up to the top.

6 Gently pour the soufflé mixture into the prepared dish and bake for 25–30 minutes until puffed and golden brown. Serve immediately.

Make sure everyone is seated before the soufflé comes out of the oven because it will begin to deflate almost immediately. This recipe works equally well with strong blue cheeses such as Roquefort.

Country-style Pâté with Leeks
Pâté de Porc aux Poireaux

1 Cut the leeks lengthways, wash well and slice thinly. Melt the butter in a large heavy pan, add the leeks, then cover and gently cook for 10 minutes, stirring occasionally. Add the garlic and continue cooking for 10 minutes until the leeks are very soft, then set aside to cool.

2 Cut the pork into 3.5cm/1¾in cubes. Working in two or three batches, put the meat into a food processor fitted with the metal blade; the bowl should be about half-full. Pulse to chop the meat to a coarse purée. Alternatively, pass the meat through the coarse blade of a meat mincer. Transfer the meat to a mixing bowl and remove any white stringy bits.

3 Reserve two of the bacon rashers for garnishing, and chop or grind the remainder. Add the bacon to the pork in the bowl.

4 Preheat the oven to 180°C/350°F/Gas 4. Line the base and sides of a 1.5 litre/2½ pint/6¼ cup terrine or loaf tin (pan) with baking parchment.

5 Add the leeks, herbs, spices and salt and pepper to the bowl with the pork and bacon and, using your fingertips, mix until well combined.

6 Spoon the mixture into the terrine or loaf tin, pressing it into the corners. Tap firmly to settle the mixture and smooth the top. Arrange the bay leaf and bacon rashers on top, then cover tightly with foil.

7 Place the terrine or loaf tin in a roasting pan and pour boiling water to come halfway up the sides. Bake for 1¼ hours.

8 Lift the terrine or tin out of the roasting pan and pour out the water. Put the terrine back in the roasting pan and place a baking sheet on top. If the pâté has not risen above the sides of the terrine, place a foil-covered board directly on the pâté. Weight with two or three large cans or other heavy objects while it cools. (Liquid will seep out which is why the terrine should stand inside a roasting tin.) Chill until cold, preferably overnight, before slicing.

Serves 8–10

450g/1lb trimmed leeks (white and light green parts)
15g/½oz/1 tbsp butter
2 or 3 large garlic cloves, finely chopped
1kg/2¼lb lean pork leg or shoulder
150g/5oz smoked rindless streaky (fatty) bacon rashers (strips)
7.5ml/1½ tsp chopped fresh thyme
3 sage leaves, finely chopped
1.5ml/¼ tsp *quatre èpices* (a mix of ground cloves, cinnamon, nutmeg and pepper)
1.5ml/¼ tsp ground cumin
pinch of freshly grated nutmeg
2.5ml/½ tsp salt
5ml/1 tsp freshly ground black pepper
1 bay leaf, to garnish

Traditionally this sort of pork pâté (or more correctly, terrine, since it has no crust) contains pork liver and egg to bind. This version uses leeks instead for a fresher flavour and a lighter result.

French Scalloped Potatoes
Pommes de Terre Dauphinoise

Serves 6

1kg/2¼lb potatoes, cut into
    2.5mm/¼ in slices
900ml/1½ pints/3⅔ cups milk
pinch of freshly grated nutmeg
1 bay leaf
15–30ml/1–2 tbsp butter, softened
2 or 3 garlic cloves, very finely
    chopped
45–60ml/3–4 tbsp crème fraîche or
    whipping cream (optional)
salt and freshly ground black pepper

COOK'S TIP
If cooked ahead, this dish will keep hot in a low oven for an hour or so; moisten the top with a little extra cream, if you like.

These potatoes taste far richer than you would expect even with only a little cream – they are delicious with just about everything, but in France, they are nearly always served with roast lamb.

1 Preheat the oven to 180°C/350°F/Gas 4.

2 Put the potatoes in a large pan and pour over the milk, to cover them. Add the salt and pepper, nutmeg and the bay leaf. Bring slowly to the boil and simmer for 15 minutes until the potatoes just start to soften, but are not completely cooked, and the milk has thickened.

3 Generously butter a 36cm/14in oval gratin dish or a 2 litre/3¼ pint/ 8 cup shallow baking dish and sprinkle the garlic over the base.

4 Using a slotted spoon, transfer the potatoes to the gratin or baking dish. Taste the milk and adjust the seasoning, then pour over enough of the milk to come just to the surface of the potatoes. Spoon a thin layer of cream over the top, or more of the thickened milk to cover.

5 Bake the potatoes for about1 hour until the milk is absorbed and the top is a deep golden brown.

Artichokes with Vinaigrette
Artichauts Vinaigrette

Serves 2

2 globe artichokes (about 250–350g/
    9–12oz each)
½ lemon

For the vinaigrette

1 shallot, very finely chopped
7.5ml/1½ tsp Dijon mustard
10ml/2 tsp lemon juice
30ml/2 tbsp extra virgin olive oil
30ml/2 tbsp vegetable oil
salt and freshly ground black pepper

The French enjoy artichokes prepared in many different ways. Simply cooked and eaten leaf by leaf is one of the best ways to savour the delicate flavour of the large Brittany artichokes.

1 Cut off about 4cm/1½in from the top of each artichoke. Using kitchen scissors, trim the tops of the remaining leaves to remove the sharp points and browned edges. Rub the cut surfaces with lemon juice to prevent discoloration, then cut the stem level with the base.

2 Place each artichoke upside down in a large pan of simmering water. Place a heatproof plate on top of the artichokes to prevent them from righting themselves. Cover and simmer for 30 minutes.

3 Remove the artichokes and allow to cool slightly, then, using a small sharp spoon, scrape out the 'choke' (the prickly inner leaves and the fuzzy layer underneath).

4 To make the vinaigrette, place all the ingredients in a small bowl and whisk until the mixture has thickened. Fill the centre of each artichoke with the vinaigrette and serve.

Mussels Steamed in White Wine
Moules Marinières

Serves 4

2kg/4½lb mussels
300ml/½ pint/1¼ cups dry white
   wine
4–6 large shallots, finely chopped
bouquet garni
freshly ground black pepper

This is the best and easiest way to serve the small tender mussels, bouchots, which are farmed along much of the French coast line. In Normandy, the local sparkling dry cider is often used instead of white wine. Serve with plenty of crusty French bread to soak up the delicious juices.

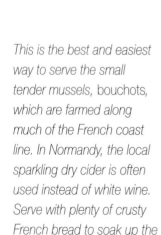

1 Discard any broken mussels and those with open shells that refuse to close when tapped. Under cold running water, scrape the mussel shells with a knife to remove any barnacles and pull out the stringy "beards". Soak the mussels in cold water for at least 1 hour.

2 In a large heavy flameproof casserole combine the wine, shallots, bouquet garni and plenty of pepper. Bring to the boil over a medium-high heat and cook for 2 minutes.

3 Add the mussels and cook, tightly covered, for 5 minutes, or until the mussels open, shaking and tossing the pan occasionally. Discard any mussels that do not open.

4 Using a slotted spoon, divide the mussels among warmed soup plates. Spoon the cooking liquid over the mussels to avoid catching any remaining sand from the mussels. Serve immediately.

Fish with Butter Sauce
Filets de Poisson Beurre Blanc

Serves 4

750g/1¾lb skinless white fish fillets, such as sole, plaice, sea bass or perch
salt and white pepper

For the butter sauce

2 shallots, finely chopped
90ml/6 tbsp white wine vinegar
15ml/1 tbsp whipping cream
175g/6oz/¾ cup unsalted (sweet) butter, cut into 12 pieces
15ml/1 tbsp chopped fresh tarragon or chives
fresh tarragon sprigs, to garnish

1 To make the sauce, put the shallots and vinegar in a small heavy pan and boil over a high heat until the liquid has almost evaporated, leaving only about 15ml/1 tbsp, then stir in the cream.

2 Reduce the heat to medium and add the butter, one piece at a time, whisking constantly until it melts before adding the next (lift the pan off the heat if the butter melts faster than it can be incorporated).

3 Season the sauce with salt and pepper to taste and whisk in the tarragon or chives. (If you prefer a smooth sauce, strain before adding the herbs.) Cover the pan and set aside in a warm place.

4 Bring some water to the boil in the bottom of a covered steamer. Season the fish fillets with salt and pepper, then steam for 3–5 minutes until the flesh is opaque. The time will depend on the thickness of the fish. Serve the fish with the sauce, garnished with fresh tarragon.

This classic French butter sauce livens up steamed or poached fish. For a dinner party, make it shortly before the guests arrive and keep warm in a vacuum flask until ready to serve.

Turbot in Parchment
Turbot en Papillote

1 Preheat the oven to 190°C/ 375°F/Gas 5. Cut four pieces of baking parchment, about 45cm/18in long. Fold each piece in half and cut into a heart shape.

2 Open the paper hearts. Arrange one quarter of each of the vegetables next to the fold of each heart. Sprinkle with salt and pepper and half the chopped herbs. Arrange two pieces of turbot fillet over each bed of vegetables, overlapping the thin end of one piece and the thicker end of the other. Sprinkle the remaining herbs, the olive oil and wine or stock evenly over the fish.

3 Fold the top half of one of the paper hearts over the fish and vegetables and, beginning at the rounded end, fold the edges of the paper over, twisting and folding to form an airtight packet. Repeat with the remaining three. (The parcels may be assembled up to 4 hours ahead and chilled.)

4 Slide the parcels on to one or two baking sheets and bake for about 10 minutes, or until the paper is lightly browned and well puffed. Slide each parcel on to a warmed plate and serve immediately.

Serves 4

2 carrots, cut into thin julienne strips

2 courgettes (zucchini), cut into thin julienne strips

2 leeks, cut into thin julienne strips

1 fennel bulb, cut into thin julienne strips

2 tomatoes, peeled, seeded and diced

30ml/2 tbsp chopped fresh dill, tarragon, or chervil

4 turbot fillets (about 200g/7oz each), cut in half

20ml/4 tsp olive oil

60ml/4 tbsp white wine or fish stock

salt and freshly ground black pepper

Cooking in paper parcels is not new, but it is an ideal way to cook fish. Serve this dish on its own or with a little hollandaise sauce and let each person open their own parcel to savour the aroma.

Pan-fried Sole Sole Meunière

1 Rinse the fish fillets under cold running water and lightly pat dry using kitchen paper.

2 Put the milk into a shallow dish about the same size as a fish fillet. Put the flour in another shallow dish and season with salt and freshly ground black pepper.

3 Heat the oil in a large frying pan over a medium-high heat and add the butter. Dip a fish fillet into the milk, then into the flour, turning to coat well, then shake off the excess.

4 Put the coated fillets into the pan in a single layer. (Do not crowd the pan; cook in batches, if necessary and keep the cooked fillets warm.) Fry the fish fillets gently for 3–4 minutes until lightly browned, turning once.

5 Sprinkle the fish with chopped parsley and serve immediately with wedges of lemon.

Serves 2
340g/¾lb skinless Dover sole or
    lemon sole fillets
125ml/4fl oz/½ cup milk
55g/2oz/⅓ cup plain (all-purpose)
    flour
15ml/1 tbsp vegetable oil, plus more
    if needed
15g/½oz/1 tbsp butter
15ml/1 tbsp chopped fresh parsley
salt and freshly ground black pepper
lemon wedges, to serve

This classic bistro recipe is perfect for fresh Dover sole and makes the most of its delicate flavour. As it is a firm, flat fish Dover sole is ideal for pan frying. Lemon sole fillets are a less expensive but equally tasty alternative.

Mediterranean Fish Stew Bouillabaisse

Serves 8

2.5kg/6lb white fish
45ml/3 tbsp extra virgin olive oil
grated rind (zest) of 1 orange
1 garlic clove, very finely chopped
pinch of saffron threads
30ml/2 tbsp pastis (anise liqueur)
1 small fennel bulb, finely chopped
1 large onion, finely chopped
225g/½lb small new potatoes, sliced
900g/2lb large raw Mediterranean
    prawns (shrimp), peeled
croûtons, to serve

For the stock

1–1.3kg/2–3lb fish heads and bones
30ml/2 tbsp olive oil
2 leeks, sliced
1 onion, halved and sliced
1 red (bell) pepper, cored and sliced
675g/1½lb ripe tomatoes, quartered
4 garlic cloves, sliced
bouquet garni
rind (zest) of ½ orange

For the rouille

30g/1oz/⅔ cup white breadcrumbs
1 or 2 garlic cloves, finely chopped
½ red (bell) pepper, roasted
5ml/1 tsp tomato purée (paste)
125ml/4fl oz/½ cup extra virgin
    olive oil

1 Cut the fish fillets into serving pieces, and reserve the trimmings for the stock. Put the fish in a bowl with 30ml/2 tbsp of the olive oil, the orange rind, garlic, saffron and pastis. Turn to coat well, cover and chill.

2 To make the stock, rinse the fish heads and bones in cold water. Heat the olive oil in a large pan or flameproof casserole. Add the leeks, onion and pepper and cook gently for 5 minutes until the onion starts to soften. Add the fish heads, tomatoes, garlic, bouquet garni, orange rind, and enough cold water to cover the ingredients by 2.5cm/1in.

3 Bring to the boil, skimming any foam that rises to the surface, then reduce the heat and simmer, covered, for 30 minutes, skimming once or twice more. Strain the stock.

4 To make the *rouille*, soak the breadcrumbs in water then squeeze dry. Put the breadcrumbs in a food processor with the garlic, roasted red pepper and tomato purée and process until smooth. With the machine running, slowly pour the oil through the feed tube, scraping down the sides once or twice.

5 To finish the bouillabaise, heat the remaining 15ml/1 tbsp of olive oil in a wide flameproof casserole over a medium heat. Cook the fennel and onion for 5 minutes until the onion softens, then add the stock. Bring to the boil, add the potatoes and cook for 5–7 minutes. Reduce the heat and add the fish, starting with the thickest pieces and adding the thinner ones after 2 or 3 minutes. Add the prawns and continue simmering gently until all the fish and shellfish is cooked.

6 Adjust the seasoning and ladle the soup into warmed bowls. Serve with croûtons spread with rouille.

Different variations of bouillabaisse abound along the Mediterranean coast and almost any combination of fish and shellfish can be used.

Old-fashioned Chicken Fricassée
Fricassée de Poulet

Serves 4–6

1.2–1.3kg/2½–3lb chicken pieces
55g/2oz/4 tbsp butter
30ml/2 tbsp vegetable oil
30g/1oz/3 tbsp plain (all-purpose) flour
250ml/8fl oz/1 cup dry white wine
750ml/1¼ pints/3 cups chicken stock
bouquet garni
1.5ml/¼ tsp white pepper
225g/8oz button (white) mushrooms, trimmed
5ml/1 tsp lemon juice
16–24 small white onions, peeled
125ml/4fl oz/½ cup water
90ml/6 tbsp whipping cream
salt
30ml/2 tbsp fresh parsley, to garnish

A fricassée is a classic dish in which poultry or meat is first seared in fat, then braised with liquid until cooked. This recipe is finished with a little cream – leave it out if you wish.

1 Wash the chicken pieces, then pat dry with kitchen paper. Melt half the butter with the oil in a large, heavy flameproof casserole. Add half the chicken pieces and cook for 10 minutes, until just golden in colour. Transfer to a plate, then cook the remaining pieces in the same way.

2 Return the seared chicken pieces to the casserole. Sprinkle with the flour, turning the pieces to coat. Cook over a low heat for about 4 minutes, turning occasionally.

3 Pour in the wine, bring to the boil and add the stock. Push the chicken pieces to one side and scrape the base of the casserole, stirring until well blended.

4 Bring the liquid to the boil, add the bouquet garni and season with a pinch of salt and white pepper. Cover and simmer over a medium heat for 25–30 minutes until the chicken is tender and the juices run clear when the thickest part of the meat is pierced with a knife.

5 Meanwhile, in a frying pan, melt the remaining butter. Add the trimmed mushrooms and lemon juice and cook for 3–4 minutes until the mushrooms are golden, stirring. Transfer the mushrooms to a bowl, add the onions and water to the pan. Simmer for about 10 minutes, until just tender. Tip the onions and any juices into the bowl with the mushrooms and set aside.

6 When the chicken is cooked, transfer the pieces to a deep serving dish and cover with foil to keep warm. Discard the bouquet garni. Add any cooking juices from the vegetables to the casserole. Bring to the boil and boil, stirring frequently, until the sauce is reduced by half.

7 Whisk the cream into the sauce and cook for 2 minutes. Add the mushrooms and onions and cook for 2 more minutes. Adjust the seasoning, pour the sauce over the chicken and sprinkle with parsley.

Chicken with Garlic Poulet à l'Ail

1 Preheat the oven to 190ºC/375ºF/ Gas 5. Pat the chicken pieces dry and season with salt and pepper.

2 Put the chicken, skin side down in a large flameproof casserole and set over a medium-high heat. Turn frequently and transfer the chicken to a plate when browned. Cook in batches if necessary and pour off the fat after browning.

3 Add the onion and garlic to the casserole and cook over a medium-low heat, covered, until lightly browned, stirring frequently.

4 Add the wine to the casserole, bring to the boil and return the chicken to the casserole. Add the stock and herbs and bring back to the boil. Cover and transfer to the oven. Cook for 25 minutes, or until the chicken is tender and the juices run clear when the thickest part of the thigh is pierced with a knife.

5 Remove the chicken pieces from the pan and strain the cooking liquid. Discard the herbs, transfer the solids to a food processor and purée until smooth. Remove any fat from the cooking liquid and return to the casserole. Stir in the garlic and onion purée, return the chicken pieces to the casserole and reheat gently for approximately 3–4 minutes before serving.

Serves 8

2kg/4½lb chicken pieces
1 large onion, halved and sliced
3 large garlic bulbs (about 200g/7oz), separated into cloves and peeled
150ml/¼ pint/⅔ cup dry white wine
175ml/6fl oz/¾ cup chicken stock
4–5 thyme sprigs, or 2.5ml/½ tsp dried thyme
1 small rosemary sprig, or a pinch of ground rosemary
1 bay leaf
salt and freshly ground black pepper

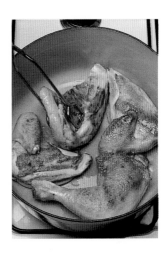

Use fresh new season's garlic if you can find it – there's no need to peel the cloves if the skin is not papery. In France, sometimes the cooked garlic cloves are spread on toasted country bread.

Chicken Braised in Red Wine Coq au Vin

Serves 4

1.6–1.8kg/3½–4lb chicken, cut
  in pieces
25ml/1½ tbsp olive oil
225g/½lb baby onions
15g/½oz/1 tbsp butter
225g/½lb mushrooms, quartered if
  large
30ml/2 tbsp plain (all-purpose) flour
750ml/1¼ pints/3 cups dry red wine
250ml/8fl oz/1 cup chicken stock, or
  more to cover
bouquet garni
salt and freshly ground black pepper

1 Pat the chicken pieces dry and season with salt and pepper. Put the chicken in a large heavy frying pan, skin side down, and cook over a medium-high heat for 10–12 minutes, or until golden brown. Transfer to a plate.

2 Meanwhile, heat the oil in a large flameproof casserole over a medium-low heat, add the onions and cook, covered, until evenly browned, stirring frequently.

3 In a heavy frying pan, melt the butter over a medium heat and sauté the mushrooms, stirring, until golden brown.

4 Sprinkle the onions with flour and cook for 2 minutes, stirring frequently, then add the wine and boil for 1 minute, stirring. Add the chicken, mushrooms, stock and bouquet garni. Bring to the boil, reduce the heat to very low and simmer, covered, for 45–50 minutes until the chicken is tender and the juices run clear when the thickest part of the meat is pierced with a knife. (Alternatively, bake in a preheated oven 170°C/325°F/Gas 3 for the same amount of time.)

5 Transfer the chicken pieces and vegetables to a plate. Strain the cooking liquid, skim off the fat and return the liquid to the pan. Boil to reduce by one-third, then return the chicken and vegetables to the casserole and simmer for 3–4 minutes to heat through.

COOK'S TIP

Avoid large flat mushrooms – although they have a lovely flavour, they will make the sauce murky.

This classic dish was originally made with an old rooster, marinated then slowly braised until very tender. White wine may be used instead of red – as in Alsace, where the local riesling is used.

Serves 4

1.2–1.3kg/2½–3lb guinea fowl
15ml/1 tbsp vegetable oil
15g/½oz/1 tbsp butter
1 large onion, halved and sliced
1 large carrot, halved and sliced
1 large leek, sliced
450g/1lb green cabbage, such as
    savoy, sliced or chopped
125ml/4fl oz/½ cup dry white wine
125ml/4fl oz/½ cup chicken stock
1 or 2 garlic cloves, finely chopped
salt and freshly ground black pepper

Guinea Fowl with Cabbage
Pintade au Chou

1 Preheat the oven to 180°C/350°F/ Gas 4. Tie the legs of the guinea fowl with string.

2 Heat half the oil in a large flameproof casserole over a medium-high heat and cook the guinea fowl until golden brown on all sides. Transfer to a plate.

3 Pour out the fat from the casserole and add the remaining oil with the butter. Add the onion, carrot and leek and cook over a low heat, stirring occasionally, for 5 minutes. Add the cabbage and cook for about 3–4 minutes until slightly wilted, stirring occasionally. Season the vegetables with salt and pepper.

4 Place the guinea fowl on its side on the vegetables. Add the wine and bring to the boil, then add the stock and garlic. Cover and transfer to the oven. Cook for 25 minutes, then turn the bird on to the other side and cook for 20–25 minutes until it is tender and the juices run clear when the thickest part of the thigh is pierced with a knife.

5 Transfer the bird to a board and leave to stand for 5–10 minutes, then cut into four or eight pieces. With a slotted spoon, transfer the cabbage to a warmed serving dish and place the guinea fowl on top. Skim any fat from the cooking juices and serve separately.

COOK'S TIP
Guinea fowl works well with any strong-tasting vegetable such as curly kale.

Guinea fowl is a domesticated relative of pheasant, so you can substitute pheasant or even chicken in this recipe. In some parts of France, such as Burgundy, garlic sausage may be added.

Rack of Lamb with Mustard
Carré d'Agneau à la Moutarde

1 Preheat the oven to 220°C/425°F/Gas 7. Trim any remaining fat from the lamb, including the fat covering over the meat.

2 In a food processor fitted with the metal blade, with the machine running, drop the garlic through the feed tube and process until finely chopped. Add the bread, herbs, mustard and a little pepper and process until combined, then slowly pour in the oil.

3 Press the mixture on to the meaty side and ends of the racks, completely covering the surface.

4 Put the racks in a shallow roasting pan, and roast for about 25 minutes for medium-rare or 3–5 minutes more for medium (a meat thermometer inserted into the thickest part of the meat should register 57–60°C/135–140°F for medium-rare to medium).

5 Transfer the meat to a carving board or warmed platter. Cut down between the bones to carve into chops. Serve garnished with rosemary and accompanied by new potatoes.

COOK'S TIP
To French trim your own rack of lamb, cut the fat around each bone down to the meat. Scrape the bones of all sinew and fat. Cut between the bones and through the eye of the lamb, leaving 1cm/ ⅓ in of meat still attached at the bottom.

This recipe is perfect for entertaining. You can coat the lamb with the crust before your guests arrive, and put it in the oven when you sit down for the first course.

Serves 6–8

3 racks of lamb (7–8 ribs each), trimmed of fat, bones 'French' trimmed
2 or 3 garlic cloves
120g/4oz (about 4 slices) white or wholemeal (whole-wheat) bread, torn into pieces
25ml/1½ tbsp fresh thyme leaves or 15ml/1 tbsp rosemary leaves
25ml/1½ tbsp Dijon mustard
freshly ground black pepper
30ml/2 tbsp olive oil
fresh rosemary, to garnish
new potatoes, to serve

Roast Leg of Lamb with Beans
Gigot d' Agneau

1 Preheat the oven to 220°C/ 425°F/Gas 7. Wipe the leg of lamb with damp kitchen paper and dry the fat covering well. Cut 2 or 3 of the garlic cloves into 10–12 slivers, then with the tip of a knife, cut 10–12 slits into the lamb and insert the garlic slivers into the slits. Rub with oil, season with salt and pepper and sprinkle with rosemary.

2 Set the lamb on a rack in a shallow roasting pan and put in the oven. After 15 minutes, reduce the heat to 180°C/350°F/Gas 4 and continue roasting for 1½–1¾ hours (about 18 minutes per 450g/1lb) or until a meat thermometer inserted into the thickest part of the meat registers 57–60°C/135–140°F for medium-rare to medium meat or 66°C/150°F for well-done.

3 Meanwhile, rinse the beans and put in a pan with enough fresh water to cover generously. Add the remaining garlic and the bay leaf, then bring to the boil. Reduce the heat and simmer for 45 minutes–1 hour, or until tender.

4 Transfer the roast to a board and stand, loosely covered, for 10–15 minutes. Skim off the fat from the cooking juices, then add the wine and stock to the roasting pan. Boil over a medium heat, stirring and scraping the base of the pan, until slightly reduced. Strain into a warmed gravy boat.

5 Drain the beans, discard the bay leaf, then toss the beans with the butter until it melts and season with salt and pepper. Garnish the lamb with watercress and serve with the beans and the sauce.

Serves 8–10

2.7–3kg/6–7lb leg of lamb
3 or 4 garlic cloves
olive oil
fresh or dried rosemary leaves
450g/1lb dried haricot (navy),
　flageolet or cannellini beans,
　soaked overnight in cold water
1 bay leaf
30ml/2 tbsp red wine
150ml/¼ pint/⅔ cup lamb stock
30g/1oz/2 tbsp butter
salt and freshly ground black pepper
watercress, to garnish

Leg of lamb is the classic Sunday roast. In France, the shank bone is not removed, but it is cut through for easier handling. The roast is often served with haricot (navy) or flageolet beans.

Pepper Steak Steak au Poivre

1 Place the peppercorns in a sturdy polythene bag. Crush with a rolling pin until medium-coarse. Alternatively you can use the flat base of a small heavy pan to press down on the peppercorns, rocking the pan to crush them.

2 Put the steaks on a board and trim away any extra fat. Press the pepper on to both sides of the meat, coating it completely.

3 Melt the butter with the oil in a heavy frying pan over a medium-high heat. Add the meat and cook for 6–7 minutes, turning once, until done as preferred (medium-rare meat will still be slightly soft when pressed, medium will be springy and well-done firm). Transfer the steaks to a warmed platter or plates and cover to keep warm.

4 Pour in the brandy to deglaze the pan. Allow to boil until reduced by half, scraping the base of the pan, then add the cream and garlic. Boil gently over a medium heat for about 4 minutes until the cream has reduced by one-third.

5 Stir any accumulated juices from the meat into the sauce, taste and add salt, if necessary, then serve the steaks with the sauce.

Serves 2

30ml/2 tbsp black peppercorns
2 fillet (beef tenderloin) or sirloin
  steaks, about 225g/8oz each
15g/½oz/1 tbsp butter
10ml/2 tsp vegetable oil
45ml/3 tbsp brandy
150ml/¼ pint/⅔ cup whipping cream
1 garlic clove, finely chopped
salt, if needed

There are many versions of this French bistro classic; some omit the cream, but it helps to balance the heat of the pepper. For the best results, use fairly thick steaks, such as lean sirloin.

Burgundy Beef Stew Boeuf Bourguignon

Serves 6

1.5kg/3½lb lean stewing beef (chuck or shin)

175g/6oz lean salt pork or thick-cut rindless streaky (fatty) bacon

40g/1½oz/3 tbsp butter

350g/12oz baby onions

350g/12oz small button (white) mushrooms

1 onion, finely chopped

1 carrot, finely chopped

2 or 3 garlic cloves, finely chopped

45ml/3 tbsp plain (all-purpose) flour

750ml/1¼ pints/3 cups red wine, preferably Burgundy

25ml/1½ tbsp tomato purée (paste)

bouquet garni

600–750ml/1–1¼ pints/2½–3 cups beef stock

15ml/1 tbsp chopped fresh parsley

salt and freshly ground black pepper

Tradition dictates that you should use the same wine in this stew that you plan to serve with it, but a less expensive full-bodied wine will do for cooking. The stew reheats very well.

1 Cut the beef into 5cm/2in pieces and dice the salt pork or cut the bacon crossways into thin strips.

2 In a large heavy flameproof casserole, cook the pork or bacon over a medium heat until golden brown, then remove with a slotted spoon and drain. Pour off all but 30ml/2 tbsp of the fat.

3 Increase the heat to medium-high. Add enough meat to the pan to fit easily in one layer (do not crowd the pan or the meat will not brown) and cook, turning to colour all sides, until well browned. Transfer the beef to a plate and continue browning the meat in batches.

4 In a heavy frying pan, melt one-third of the butter over a medium heat, add the baby onions and cook, stirring frequently, until evenly golden. Set aside on a plate.

5 In the same pan, melt half of the remaining butter over a medium heat. Add the mushrooms and sauté, stirring frequently, until golden, then set aside with the baby onions.

6 When all the beef has been browned, pour off any fat from the casserole and add the remaining butter. When the butter has melted, add the onion, carrot and garlic and cook over a medium heat for 3–4 minutes until just softened, stirring frequently. Sprinkle over the flour and cook for 2 minutes, then add the wine, tomato purée and bouquet garni. Bring to the boil, scraping the base of the pan.

7 Return the beef and bacon to the casserole and pour on the stock, adding more if needed to cover the meat and vegetables when pressed down. Cover the casserole and simmer very gently over a low heat, stirring occasionally, for about 3 hours or until the meat is very tender. Add the sautéed mushrooms and baby onions and cook, covered, for a further 30 minutes. Discard the bouquet garni and stir in the parsley before serving.

Toulouse Cassoulet *Cassoulet*

Serves 6–8

450g/1lb dried haricot (navy) or
    cannellini beans, soaked overnight
    in cold water, then rinsed and
    drained
675g/1½lb Toulouse sausages
550g/1¼lb each boneless lamb and
    pork shoulder, cut into 5cm/2in
    pieces
1 large onion, finely chopped
3 or 4 garlic cloves, very finely
    chopped
4 tomatoes, peeled, seeded and
    chopped
300ml/½ pint/1¼ cups chicken
    stock
bouquet garni
60ml/4 tbsp fresh breadcrumbs
salt and freshly ground black pepper

1 Put the beans in a pan with water to cover. Boil vigorously for 10 minutes and drain, then return to a clean pan, cover with water and bring to the boil. Reduce the heat and simmer for 45 minutes, or until tender, then add a little salt and leave to soak in the cooking water.

2 Preheat the oven to 180°C/ 350°F/Gas 4. Prick the sausages, place them in a large heavy frying pan over a medium heat and cook for 20–25 minutes until browned, turning occasionally. Drain on kitchen paper and pour off all but 15ml/1 tbsp of the fat from the pan.

3 Increase the heat to medium-high. Season the lamb and pork and add enough of the meat to the pan to fit easily in one layer. Cook until browned, then transfer to a large dish. Continue browning in batches.

4 Add the onion and garlic to the pan and cook for 3–4 minutes until just soft, stirring. Stir in the tomatoes and cook for 2–3 minutes, then transfer the vegetables to the meat dish. Add the stock and bring to the boil, then skim off the fat.

5 Spoon a quarter of the beans into a large casserole, and top with a third of the sausages, meat and vegetables.

6 Continue layering, ending with a layer of beans. Tuck in the bouquet garni, pour over the stock and top up with enough of the bean cooking liquid to just cover.

7 Cover the casserole and bake for 2 hours (check and add more bean cooking liquid if it seems dry). Uncover the casserole, sprinkle over the breadcrumbs and press with the back of a spoon to moisten them. Continue cooking the cassoulet, uncovered, for about 20 minutes more until browned.

There are as many versions of this regional speciality in
South-west France as there are towns.

Upside-down Apple Tart Tarte Tatin

Serves 8–10

plain (all-purpose) flour
225g/½lb puff or shortcrust pastry
10–12 large Golden Delicious apples
  lemon juice
120g/4oz/½ cup unsalted butter, cut
  into pieces
120g/4oz/½ cup caster (superfine)
  sugar
2.5ml/½ tsp ground cinnamon
crème fraîche or whipped cream, to
  serve

1 On a lightly floured surface, roll out the pastry into a 28cm/11in round less than 6mm/¼in thick. Transfer to a lightly floured baking sheet and chill.

2 Peel the apples, cut them in half lengthways and core. Sprinkle the apples generously with lemon juice.

3 In a 25cm/10in *tarte tatin* tin (tart pan), cook the butter, sugar and cinnamon over a medium heat until the butter has melted and sugar dissolved, stirring occasionally. Continue cooking for 6–8 minutes, until the mixture turns a medium caramel colour, then remove the tin from the heat and arrange the apple halves, standing on their edges, in the tin, fitting them in tightly since they shrink during cooking.

4 Return the apple-filled tin to the heat and bring to a simmer over a medium heat for 20–25 minutes until the apples are tender and coloured. Remove the tin from the heat and cool slightly.

5 Preheat the oven to 230°C/ 450°F/Gas 8. Place the pastry on top of the apple-filled tin and tuck the edges of the pastry inside the edge of the tin around the apples. Pierce the pastry in two or three places, then bake for 25–30 minutes until the pastry is golden and the filling is bubbling. Leave to cool in the tin for 10–15 minutes.

6 To serve, run a sharp knife around edge of the tin to loosen the pastry. Cover with a serving plate and, holding them tightly, carefully invert the tin and plate together (do this carefully, preferably over the sink in case any caramel drips). Lift off the tin and loosen any apples that stick with a palette knife. Serve the tart warm with cream.

This tart was first made by two sisters who served it in their restaurant near Sologne in the Loire Valley. A special tarte tatin tin is ideal, but an ovenproof frying pan will do very well.

Crêpes with Orange Sauce Crêpes Suzette

Serves 6

120g/40z/⅔ cup plain (all-purpose) flour
1.5ml/¼ tsp salt
30g/1oz/2 tbsp caster (superfine) sugar
2 eggs, lightly beaten
250ml/8fl oz/1 cup milk
60ml/4 tbsp water
30ml/2 tbsp orange flower water or orange liqueur (optional)
30g/1oz/2 tbsp unsalted (sweet) butter, melted, plus more for frying

For the orange sauce

85g/3oz/6 tbsp unsalted (sweet) butter
55g/2oz/¼ cup caster (superfine) sugar
grated rind (zest) and juice of 1 large unwaxed orange
grated rind (zest) and juice of 1 unwaxed lemon
150ml/¼ pint/⅔ cup fresh orange juice
60ml/4 tbsp orange liqueur, plus extra for flaming (optional)
brandy, for flaming (optional)
orange segments, to decorate

1 In a bowl, sift together the flour, salt and sugar. Make a well in the centre and pour in the eggs. Beat the eggs, bringing in a little flour until it is all incorporated. Slowly whisk in the milk and water to make a smooth batter. Whisk in the orange flower water or liqueur, if using, then strain the batter into a bowl and set aside for 20–30 minutes.

2 Heat a 18–20cm/7–8in crêpe pan over a medium heat. Stir the melted butter into the crêpe batter. Brush the hot pan with a little melted butter and pour in about 30ml/2 tbsp of batter. Quickly tilt and rotate the pan to cover the base with a thin layer of batter. Cook for about 1 minute until the top is set and the base is golden. Carefully turn over the crêpe and cook for 20–30 seconds. Tip out on to a plate.

3 Continue cooking the crêpes, brushing the pan with a little melted butter as and when necessary. Place a sheet of clear film (plastic wrap) between the crêpes as they are stacked to prevent sticking.

4 To make the sauce, melt the butter in a large frying pan over a medium-low heat, then stir in the sugar, orange and lemon rind and juice, the additional orange juice and the orange liqueur.

5 Place a crêpe in the pan browned-side down, swirling gently to coat with the sauce. Fold it in half, then in half again to form a triangle and push to the side of the pan. Continue heating and folding the crêpes until all are warm and covered with the sauce.

6 To flame the crêpes, heat 30–45ml/2–3 tbsp each of orange liqueur and brandy in a small pan over a medium heat. Remove the pan from the heat, carefully ignite the liquid with a match then gently pour over the crêpes. Sprinkle over the orange segments and serve immediately.

This is one of the best-known French desserts. You can make the crêpes in advance, then you will be able to put the dish together quickly at the last minute.

Chocolate Mousse Mousse au Chocolat Amer

Serves 8

225g/8oz plain (semisweet)
    chocolate, chopped
60ml/4 tbsp water
30ml/2 tbsp orange liqueur or brandy
30g/1oz/2 tbsp unsalted (sweet)
    butter, cut into small pieces
4 eggs, separated
90ml/6 tbsp whipping cream
1.5ml/¼ tsp cream of tartar
45ml/3 tbsp caster (superfine) sugar

This is the quintessential French dessert – easy to prepare ahead, rich and extremely moreish. Use the darkest chocolate you can find for the best and most intense chocolate flavour.

1 Place the chocolate and water in a heavy pan. Melt over a low heat, stirring until smooth. Remove the pan from the heat and whisk in the liqueur and butter.

2 With an electric mixer, beat the egg yolks for 2–3 minutes until thick and creamy, then slowly beat into the melted chocolate until well blended. Set aside. Whip the cream until soft peaks form and stir a spoonful into the chocolate mixture to lighten it. Fold in the remaining cream.

3 In a clean greasefree bowl, using an electric mixer, beat the egg whites slowly until frothy. Add the cream of tartar, increase the speed and continue beating until they form soft peaks. Gradually sprinkle over the sugar and continue beating until the whites are stiff and glossy.

4 Using a rubber spatula, stir one-quarter of the egg whites into the chocolate mixture, then gently fold in the remaining whites, cutting down to the bottom, along the sides and up to the top until they are just combined. Gently spoon into a 2 litre/3¼ pint/8 cup dish or into eight individual dishes. Chill for at least 2 hours until set.

Baked Custard with Burnt Sugar Crème Brûlée

Serves 6

1 vanilla pod (bean)

1 litre/1⅔ pints/4 cups double (heavy) cream

6 egg yolks

100g/3½oz/½ cup caster (superfine) sugar

30ml/2 tbsp almond or orange liqueur

85g/3oz/⅓ cup soft light brown sugar

1 Preheat the oven to 150°C/300°F/ Gas 2. Place six 125ml/4fl oz/ ½ cup ramekins in a roasting pan or ovenproof dish and set aside.

2 Split the vanilla pod lengthways and scrape the seeds into a pan. Add the cream and gently bring just to the boil, stirring frequently. Remove from the heat and cover. Set aside to stand for 15–20 minutes.

3 In a bowl, whisk the egg yolks, sugar and liqueur until well blended. Whisk in the cream and strain. Divide the custard among the ramekins.

4 Pour enough boiling water into the roasting pan to come halfway up the sides of the ramekins. Cover the pan with foil and bake for 30 minutes until the custards are set. Remove from the pan and cool.

5 Preheat the grill (broiler). Sprinkle the sugar evenly over the surface of each custard and grill (broil) for 30–60 seconds until the sugar melts and caramelizes. (Do not allow the sugar to burn or the custard to curdle.) Place in the refrigerator to set the crust and chill completely before serving.

This dessert is widely served in cafes and restaurants throughout France. Add a little liqueur to the mixture, if you like, but it is equally delicious without it.

Chocolate Profiteroles Profiteroles au Chocolat

Serves 4–6

275g/10oz plain (semisweet)
    chocolate
120ml/8 tbsp warm water
750ml/1¼ pints/3 cups vanilla ice
    cream

For the profiteroles

110g/3¾oz/¾ cup plain (all-
    purpose) flour
1.5ml/¼ tsp salt
pinch of freshly grated nutmeg
175ml/6fl oz/¾ cup water
85g/3oz/6 tbsp unsalted (sweet)
    butter, cut into 6 pieces
3 eggs

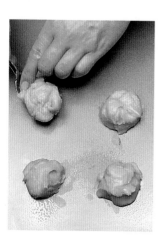

1 Preheat the oven to 200°C/400°F/ Gas 6 and butter a baking sheet.

2 To make the profiteroles, sift together the flour, salt and nutmeg. In a medium pan, bring the water and butter to the boil. Remove from the heat and add the dry ingredients. Beat with a wooden spoon for about 1 minute until well blended and the mixture starts to pull away from the sides of the pan, then set the pan over a low heat and cook the mixture for about 2 minutes, beating constantly. Remove from the heat.

3 Beat 1 egg in a small bowl and set aside. Add the remaining eggs, one at a time, to the flour mixture, beating well after each. Add the beaten egg by teaspoonfuls until the dough is smooth and shiny; it should pull away and fall slowly when dropped from a spoon.

4 Using a tablespoon, drop the dough on to the baking sheet in 12 mounds. Bake for 25–30 minutes until the pastry is well risen and browned. Turn off the oven and leave the puffs to cool with the oven door open.

5 To make the sauce, place the chocolate and water in a double-boiler or in a bowl placed over a pan of hot water and leave to melt, stirring occasionally. Keep warm until ready to serve.

6 Split the profiteroles in half and put a small scoop of ice cream in each. Arrange on a serving platter or divide among individual plates. Pour the chocolate sauce over the top and serve immediately.

This mouthwatering dessert is served in cafés throughout France. Sometimes the profiteroles are filled with whipped cream instead of ice cream, but they are always drizzled with chocolate sauce.

French Chocolate Cake Gâteau au Chocolat

Serves 10–12

150g/5oz/¾ cup caster (superfine) sugar, plus extra for sprinkling
275g/10oz plain (semisweet) chocolate, chopped
175g/6oz/¾ cup unsalted (sweet) butter, cut into pieces
10ml/2 tsp vanilla extract
5 eggs, separated
40g/1½oz/¼ cup plain (all-purpose) flour, sifted
pinch of salt
icing (confectioners') sugar, for dusting

COOK'S TIP

If the cake is baked the top should spring back if lightly touched with a fingertip. If the cake appears to rise unevenly, rotate after 20 minutes.

This is typical of a French home-made cake – dense, dark and delicious. The texture is very different from a sponge cake and it is excellent served with cream or a fruit coulis.

1 Preheat the oven to 170°C/ 325°F/Gas 3. Butter a 24cm/9½in springform tin (pan), sprinkle with a little sugar and tap out the excess.

2 Set aside 45ml/3 tbsp of the sugar. Place the chocolate, butter and remaining sugar in a heavy pan and gently cook until the chocolate and butter have melted and the sugar has dissolved. Remove the pan from the heat, stir in the vanilla extract and leave the mixture to cool slightly. Beat the egg yolks into the chocolate mixture, beating each in well, then stir in the flour.

3 In a clean greasefree bowl, using an electric mixer, beat the egg whites slowly until they are frothy. Increase the speed, add the salt and continue beating until soft peaks form. Sprinkle over the reserved sugar and beat until the whites are stiff and glossy. Beat one third of the whites into the chocolate mixture, then fold in the remaining whites. Carefully pour the mixture into the tin and tap the tin gently to release any air bubbles.

4 Bake the cake for about 35–45 minutes until well risen. Transfer the cake to a wire rack, remove the sides of the tin and cool. Remove the tin base. Dust the cake with icing sugar and transfer to a serving plate.

Nutritional notes

French Onion Soup: Energy 415kcal/1745kJ; Protein 13g; Carbohydrate 61.6g, of which sugars 12.6g; Fat 14.1g, of which saturates 6.7g; Cholesterol 25mg; Calcium 240mg; Fibre 4.1g; Sodium 1022mg.

Wild Mushroom Soup: Energy 143kcal/592kJ; Protein 3.7g; Carbohydrate 8.2g, of which sugars 3.2g; Fat 9g, of which saturates 5.3g; Cholesterol 22mg; Calcium 41mg; Fibre 2g; Sodium 174mg.

Provençal Vegetable Soup: Energy 207cal/867KJ; Protein 10.2g; Carbohydrate 20.0gm, of which sugars 5.9g; Fats 10.1gm, of which saturates 3g; Cholesterol 11.1mg; Calcium 165.0mg; Fibre 6.8g; Sodium 88mg.

Chèvre Cheese Souffle: Energy 173cal/718KJ; Protein 10.3g; Carbohydrate 5.8gm, of which sugars 1.8g; Fats 12.2gm, of which saturates 8g; Cholesterol 39.2 mg; Calcium 81.5mg; Fibre 0.2g; Sodium 279mg.

Country-style Pâté: Energy 211kcal/884kJ; Protein 27.5g; Carbohydrate 1.3g, of which sugars 1g; Fat 10.7g, of which saturates 4.4g; Cholesterol 87mg; Calcium 20mg; Fibre 1.0g; Sodium 395mg.

Scalloped Potatoes: Energy 204kcal/866kJ; Protein 8g; Carbohydrate 33.9g, of which sugars 9.2g; Fat 5.1g, of which saturates 3.1g; Cholesterol 14mg; Calcium 191mg; Fibre 1.7g; Sodium 98mg.

Artichokes: Energy 224cal/924KJ; Protein 3.4g; Carbohydrate 3.6gm, of which sugars 2.1g; Fats 22.5gm, of which saturates 3g; Cholesterol 0.0mg; Calcium 52.0mg; Fibre 0.2g; Sodium 105mg.

Mussels in White Wine: Energy 189kcal/799kJ; Protein 26.4g; Carbohydrate 2.4g, of which sugars 1.9g; Fat 3.1g, of which saturates 0.5g; Cholesterol 60mg; Calcium 308mg; Fibre 0.4g; Sodium 319mg.

Fish with Butter Sauce: Energy 559cal/2319KJ; Protein 32.0g; Carbohydrate 0.8gm, of which sugars 0.5g; Fats 47.7gm, of which saturates 30g; Cholesterol 205.2mg; Calcium 103.8mg; Fibre 0.2g; Sodium 234mg.

Turbot in Parchment: Energy 314cal/1318KJ; Protein 38.7g; Carbohydrate 16.9gm, of which sugars 15.7g; Fats 9.6gm, of which saturates 2g; Cholesterol 0.0mg; Calcium 187.3mg; Fibre 7.0g; Sodium 189mg.

Sole: Energy 218cal/914KJ; Protein 30.4g; Carbohydrate 4.3gm, of which sugars 0.4g; Fats 8.9gm, of which saturates 4g; Cholesterol 118.2mg; Calcium 55.0mg; Fibre 0.6g; Sodium 211mg.

Fish Stew: Energy 321kcal/1344kJ; Protein 46.8g; Carbohydrate 3.2g, of which sugars 2.8g; Fat 13g, of which saturates 1.9g; Cholesterol 115mg; Calcium 38mg; Fibre 1.3g; Sodium 163mg.

Chicken Fricassee: Energy 498cal/2066KJ; Protein 27.3g; Carbohydrate 10.8gm, of which sugars 5.3g; Fats 35.8gm, of which saturates 14g; Cholesterol 167.3mg; Calcium 49.2 mg; Fibre 1.5g; Sodium 291mg.

Chicken with Garlic: Energy 372cal/1548KJ; Protein 33.3g; Carbohydrate 5.8gm, of which sugars 1.6g; Fats 22.7gm, of which saturates 6g; Cholesterol 165.0mg; Calcium 27.3mg; Fibre 1.3g; Sodium 146mg.

Chicken Braised in Red Wine: Energy 774cal/3216KJ; Protein 52.3g; Carbohydrate 10.9gm, of which sugars 3.8g; Fats 44.1gm, of which saturates 13g; Cholesterol 272.0mg; Calcium 58.3mg; Fibre 1.7g; Sodium 282mg.

Guinea Fowl with Cabbage: Energy 756cal/3157KJ; Protein 87.8g; Carbohydrate 13.6gm, of which sugars 11.6g; Fats 37.1gm, of which saturates 13g; Cholesterol 660.0mg; Calcium 181.8mg; Fibre6.2g; Sodium 274mg.

Rack of Lamb with Mustard: Energy 612cal/2534KJ; Protein 36.7g; Carbohydrate 7.1gm, of which sugars 0.8g; Fats48.7gm, of which saturates 23g; Cholesterol 151.9mg; Calcium 75.1mg; Fibre 0.5g; Sodium 283mg.

Roast Leg of Lamb with Beans: Energy 563cal/2355KJ; Protein 50.1g; Carbohydrate 22.4gm, of which sugars 1.3g; Fats 30.7gm, of which saturates 10g; Cholesterol 156.6mg; Calcium 89.3mg; Fibre 7.7g; Sodium138mg.

Pepper Steak: Energy 721cal/2994KJ; Protein 54.4g; Carbohydrate 2.4gm, of which sugars 2.4g; Fats 49.3gm, of which saturates 27g; Cholesterol 209.5mg; Calcium 60.0mg; Fibre 0.0g; Sodium 228mg.

Burgundy Beef Stew: Energy 605cal/2530KJ; Protein 64.0g; Carbohydrate 13.9gm of which sugars 6.1g; Fats 23.8gm, of which saturates 10g; Cholesterol 178.2mg; Calcium 62.5mg; Fibre 2.3g; Sodium 680mg.

Cassoulet: Energy 378kcal/1586kJ; Protein 31.1g; Carbohydrate 28.5g, of which sugars 6.7g; Fat 16.5g, of which saturates 5.6g; Cholesterol 93mg; Calcium 92mg; Fibre 6.6g; Sodium 581mg.

Apple Tart: Energy 228Kcal/954kJ; Protein 1.6g; Carbohydrate 23.7g, of which sugars 15.7g; Fat 15g, of which saturates 6g; Cholesterol 25mg; Calcium 23mg; Fibre 1.1g; Sodium 141mg.

Crêpes: Energy 338cal/1411KJ; Protein 4.7g; Carbohydrate 33.3gm, of which sugars 18.0g; Fats 21.6gm, of which saturates 13g; Cholesterol 130.7mg; Calcium 50.3mg; Fibre 0.7g; Sodium36mg.

Chocolate Mousse: Energy 464kcal/1951kJ; Protein 10.6g; Carbohydrate 61.3g, of which sugars 60.9g; Fat 19.1g, of which saturates 9.1g; Cholesterol 256mg; Calcium 70mg; Fibre 1.1g; Sodium 98mg.

Baked Custard: Energy 996Kcal/4116kJ; Protein 5.7g; Carbohydrate 31.6g, of which sugars 31.6g; Fat 95g, of which saturates 57.2g; Cholesterol 430mg; Calcium 120mg; Fibre 0g; Sodium 47mg.

Profiteroles: Energy 647kcal/2707kJ; Protein 11.7g; Carbohydrate 68.2g, of which sugars 52.4g; Fat 36.9g, of which saturates 22.7g; Cholesterol 155mg; Calcium 182mg; Fibre 1.7g; Sodium 189mg.

French chocolate cake: Energy 3799kcal/15862kJ; Protein 50.6g; Carbohydrate 363.5g, of which sugars 330.6g; Fat 249.1g, of which saturates 145.2g; Cholesterol 1341mg; Calcium 400mg; Fibre 8.1g; Sodium 1437mg.

Index